REES, R.

The Victorians at work

Please return or renew this item by the last date shown.
You may renew items (unless they have been requested
by another customer) by telephoning, writing to or calling
in at any library.  100% recycled paper   *BKS 1 (5/95)*

*Life in
Victorian Britain*

The Victorians
at Work

Rosemary Rees

First published in Great Britain by Heinemann Library
an imprint of Heinemann Publishers (Oxford) Ltd
Halley Court, Jordan Hill, Oxford OX2 8EJ

MADRID ATHENS PARIS FLORENCE PRAGUE WARSAW PORTSMOUTH NH CHICAGO
SAO PAULO SINGAPORE TOKYO MELBOURNE AUCKLAND IBADAN GABORONE JOHANNESBURG

Designed by Ron Kamen, Green Door Design Ltd, Basingstoke, Hampshire
Colour Repro by Track QSP Ltd, London
Printed in Spain by Mateu Cromo Artes Graficas SA

99 98 97 96 95
10 9 8 7 6 5 4 3 2 1

ISBN 0 431 06666 3 [HB]

99 98 97 96 95
10 9 8 7 6 5 4 3 2 1

ISBN 0 431 06680 9 [PB]

British Library Cataloguing in Publication Data
Rees, Rosemary
  Victorians at Work. - (Life in Victorian Britain Series)
  I. Title II. Series
  941.081

Acknowledgements
The Publishers would like to thank the following for permission to reproduce photographs:
The Bridgeman Art Library: p. 22A
City of Aberdeen Arts and Recreation Division – Library Services: p. 9B
E.T. Archive: p. 15D
The Elton Collection: Ironbridge Gorge Museum Trust: p. 24A
Hulton Deutsch: p. 7B, p. 28A, p. 29C
The Illustrated London News Photographic Library: p. 14A
Manchester City Art Galleries: p. 5B
The Mary Evans Photographic Library: p. 13B, p. 19B, p. 25B, p. 27B
Museum in Docklands Project: p. 26A
The Science Museum/Science & Society Picture Library: p. 20A
The Sutcliffe Gallery: p. 16A

Cover photograph © The Sutcliffe Gallery

Our thanks to Professor Eric Evans of the University of Lancaster for his comments in the preparation
of this book.

Every effort has been made to contact copyright holders of any material reproduced in this book.
Any omissions will be rectified in subsequent printings if notice is given to the Publisher.

Weights, measures and money

Victorians used a system of weights and measures that is not the same as the metric system
we use now. The system the Victorians used is called the 'Imperial' system.

Imperial measures

Length
1 inch [2.5 cm]
12 inches (1 foot) [30.0 cm]
3 feet (1 yard) [1.0 m]
1,760 yards [1.6 km]

Capacity
1 pint [0.56 litres]
8 pints (1 gallon) [4.50 litres]

Weight
1 ounce (oz) [28 grams]
16 oz (1 pound 'lb') [.45 kg]
14 lbs (1 stone) [6.3 kg]
28 lbs (1 quarter) [12.75 kg]
4 qtrs (1 hundredweight 'cwt')
   [50.00 kg]
20 cwts (1 ton) [1 tonne]

Area
1 acre [0.40 hectares]

Money
4 farthings = 1 penny (1*d*)
2 halfpennies = 1 penny (1*d*)
12 pennies = 1 shilling
   (1/- or 1*s*)
20 shillings = £1

Contents

1 Victorians and work

How do we know?

Many Victorians wanted to find out as much as they could about the world around them. Some of them, for example, became explorers in Africa; others collected ancient rocks and fossils and tried to find out how old the Earth was and how it began. Some wanted to find out how poor people lived in Britain's big cities.

In 1849 Henry Mayhew (1812–87) spent months investigating how the poor people of London lived and worked. What he found out was published in a newspaper *The Morning Chronicle*. Between 1891 and 1903

Charles Booth (1840–1916) wrote seventeen books in a series called *The Life and Labour of the People of London*. At about the same time, Seebohm Rowntree (1871–1954) was finding out about poor people in York. He had the results printed in his book *Poverty*.

The government, too, conducted investigations into the ways in which people worked in mines, mills and factories. They published reports and made new laws. Every ten years there was a **census**. A census **enumerator** visited every house in the country. He wrote down things like how many children they had, whether they had any lodgers or servants and where everyone living in the house had been born.

We therefore know a lot about poor people. It is not so easy to find out about rich and middle-class people. They had to give the same sorts of information to census enumerators as poor people, but no one investigated the rest of their lives in detail. We have to rely mostly on things like letters and account books, diaries and memories, paintings and photographs.

Who did work in Victorian times?

Most people worked in Victorian times. They did different sorts of work; they worked for different lengths of time and they earned different amounts of money. Very rich people didn't work for money. They sat on committees and saw to the affairs of their country.

Source A

The queen reigns over two nations, who are as ignorant of each others' habits, thoughts and feelings, as if they were dwellers in different zones, or living on different planets, who are formed by a different breeding, who are fed by different food, are ordered by different manners, and are not governed by the same laws.

'You speak of,' said Egremont, 'the *rich* and the *poor!*'

This comes from a story called *Sybil*. It was written by Benjamin Disraeli in 1845. He was MP for Maidstone and went on to become Prime Minister. Victorian researchers found out that there were many more divisions between people apart from 'rich' and 'poor'.

They **invested** their money in industries and businesses and helped to make Britain prosperous. Their wives and daughters never worked. The middle classes worked at **respectable** jobs, which didn't involve working with their hands. Towards the end of the century, some jobs were thought suitable for middle-class women. The working classes took whatever jobs they could – digging and lifting, sweeping and scrubbing. Some were paid regularly; most earned what they could, when they could. All worked very long hours for very little money. Working-class women and children worked down mines and in mills, up chimneys and in the fields. Life for most people was a desperate struggle to work for long enough and to earn enough to keep alive.

This picture was painted by Ford Madox Brown in 1856. It shows many different kinds of work done by the Victorians. If you look carefully you will see that no one looks ill or hungry or starved or dirty.

2 Rich people at work

The aristocracy

In Victorian times there were about three hundred really rich families. The heads of these families were dukes and earls, viscounts and barons. They and their families were the **aristocracy**. They owned vast estates in the country and houses in London.

People as rich as this provided work for hundreds of poorer people. On their estates there were, for example, jobs for farm managers, gardeners, grooms and stable lads. The landowner left the day-to-day managing of his estates to a bailiff.

This meant that the landowner was free to work at whatever most interested him. He might, for example, want to work on his country's affairs in the **House of Lords**.

In rich people's houses there were jobs for valets and butlers, ladies' maids, parlour maids and scullery maids, cooks, housekeepers, nursemaids and governesses. Rich men's wives never worked for money. They made sure the household ran smoothly. They visited the poor and the sick. They entertained visitors.

This picture is called *Visiting the Poor*. It is from a book written in 1839 by Sarah Stickney Ellis.

Source A

These men are buying and selling shares
in different businesses and industries. The
picture was drawn in 1891.

The gentry

The gentry were not quite so rich, but they were
rich enough. Their estates were about 2,000 acres.
They were the local squires. They lived in
comfortable houses surrounded by gardens. They
usually owned a farm which they let to **tenant
farmers**. Like the aristocracy, they provided work for
many people on their estates. Unlike the aristocracy,
they could not afford houses in London. Instead
they stayed on their estates. They became involved
in the life of the county in which they lived.

The gentry worked, but not with their hands and
not for money. They worked on local affairs because
they felt it was their duty to do so, and because they
could influence the way things happened. Some of
them used their money to buy shares in industries
and businesses. They allowed their sons and
daughters to marry the sons and daughters of men
like **bankers** and shipowners. In this way they made
even more money and influenced the ways in
which the country became rich and prosperous.

Most days of the
week were filled with
county or parish business
– inspection of prisons,
workhouse, reformatory
schools, parish schools
and lunatic asylum; Petty
Sessions, local Board of
Health, hospital
committees, savings
bank, Provident and
Friendly societies, school
of art, Volunteer drill and
Rifle shooting.

**In 1861 Professor Von
Holltzendorff visited
England. He stayed
with a local squire,
Barwick Lloyd Baker at
Hardwicke Court in
Gloucestershire. He
wrote down all the
different jobs the
squire did.**

7

3 Mill owners and doctors

Some Victorians wrote and made speeches about the different sorts of people who lived and worked in Britain. By about 1850 they were beginning to talk about a group of people they called the 'middle class'. These middle-class people were not the **aristocracy** and gentry. They were not poor working people, either. Some middle-class people were very rich, like mill owners. Some, like railway guards, were not so well-off. The important thing about middle-class people was that they did not have to earn money by working with their hands, like dock-workers, furniture-makers and navvies.

Mill owners

The mill owners of Manchester and Bradford, the **bankers** and **merchants** of London, the **ironmasters** of Cardiff and the shipyard owners of Liverpool were all very rich men. They gave jobs to large numbers of men, women and children in their mills, mines and factories. They **invested** money in their own industries and in the industries of others. In these ways they controlled the business life of the towns and cities where they lived.

Some of these rich middle-class Victorians paid their workers as little as possible and made them work for as long as they could. Others were more thoughtful and tried to give their workers better **working conditions** while at the same time making sure their **profits** did not fall.

Doctors

In Victorian times, doctors and surgeons visited well-off people in their homes and treated them there. This was because until about 1880 there was far more danger of catching an **infection** in a hospital than at home. They treated poorer people in hospitals. Doctors and surgeons who treated the rich sent them large bills and earned a lot of money. Some doctors worked with poor people and did not earn much money.

 Source A

He hath built up a palace to Labour,
Will equal the Caesars of old;
The Church and the School and the Cottage,
And **lavished** his thousands of gold;
Where the workmen may live and be happy,
Enjoying the fruits of his hand,
Surrounded with comfort and plenty,
Secure as a **peer** of the land.

In the 1870s workmen sang this song in Bradford, Yorkshire. They were praising Titus Salt, who was a local mill owner. He moved his work people out of Bradford because he thought it was an unhealthy place in which to live and work. In 1853 he built a new mill outside Bradford which was light and airy. He built solid houses for his work people. The mill and houses made a new village which was called Saltaire.

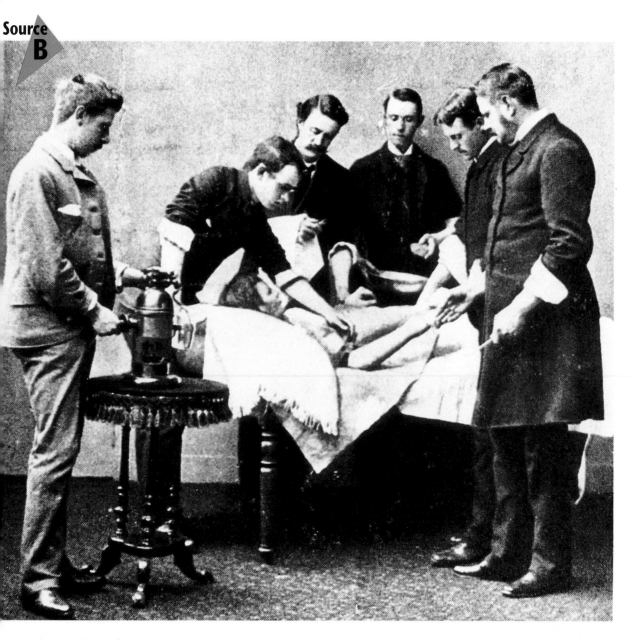

Henry Pomfret was a surgeon who lived near Manchester. In the 1840s he worked amongst the navvies who built the railway lines. You can read more about the navvies on page 20. He was paid by the navvies. They clubbed together and paid him out of their wages. Henry Pomfret did not earn much money from the navvies, but he did the work because he thought it was important.

This is a photograph of an operation taking place in the Royal Infirmary in Aberdeen in about 1870. The man on the right is working a special spray. It was invented by Joseph Lister in 1865. This sprayed dilute carbolic acid all over the patient and the doctors. The carbolic killed tiny germs which no one could see. If these germs were not killed, they would cause infections and the patient might die.

4 Railway guards and shopkeepers

Most middle-class people were not wealthy tycoons like mill owners and **ironmasters**. Most middle-class people had not been to university, like doctors and **lawyers**. Most middle-class people worked hard at **respectable** jobs. They were shopkeepers and **commercial travellers**, grocers' assistants, railway guards, post office workers and coal **merchants**. Some of them earned less than skilled workers, sometimes called artisans, who were considered by Victorians to be working class. A school teacher might earn around £60 a year in 1850. A skilled cabinet-maker would earn about £100. But the cabinet-maker was working class because he worked with his hands.

This photograph was taken at Lewisham station in 1885. Railway guards had to make sure that everyone was safely on the train and all goods were properly stowed. When the guard was sure it was safe for the train to leave the station he blew his whistle and waved his green flag to let the engine driver know that the train could move off. Guards travelled with the train and had to be alert to all kinds of danger.

Middle-class girls at work

During Queen Victoria's reign, industry grew stronger and Britain's empire grew larger. More and more people were needed to work as clerks and typists, book-keepers and telephonists. By the 1880s and 1890s Victorians thought these sorts of jobs were suitable for less well-off middle-class girls and women. The Post Office was one of the first businesses to give jobs to women. Until about 1870, it was usually men who were shop assistants. Gradually, and partly because there were more and more shops, Victorians decided that shop work was suitable for women. The work was higher in **status** than that of a factory worker. But the pay was no better and the hours were as long.

This photograph of a shop in Putney, London, was taken in the 1880s. The sign above the shop says that the owner of the shop, S. W. Lydiatt, is a 'Pork Butcher and Dairyman'. He is probably the man in dark overalls, outside the dairy side of the shop. The shop sells bread and eggs, too. Mrs Lydiatt is in the shop doorway. She is wearing a butcher's apron. There are sides of meat hanging up outside the shop window. Perhaps the people standing around on the pavement are some of Mr and Mrs Lydiatt's customers who want to be in the photograph.

Source B

5 Farmers, blacksmiths, cowmen and shepherds

The **aristocracy** and gentry owned most of the land in Britain. Of course, they didn't work in the fields themselves. Instead they let out the farms on their land to **tenant farmers**. These tenant farmers did not own the land. They paid **rent** to the aristocracy and gentry. They then farmed the land themselves with the help of their families. On larger farms, tenant farmers paid men like shepherds, cowmen and general labourers to help them.

Farmers

The tenant farmers were the middle class of the countryside. They did all sorts of farming. They kept sheep and cows; they grew wheat, oats and barley; they grew apples and hops. It all depended on what the land and **climate** were like. They made enough money to keep themselves and their families in comfortable farmhouses. Many of them earned enough money to give work to servants as well as to farmworkers.

Farmworkers

Most farmworkers did not have permanent jobs. Farmworkers with special skills, like shepherds and cowmen, and men who were expert at **hedging and ditching**, were hired for a year at a time by tenant farmers. Many of them stayed with the same tenant farmer for years and years. Some skilled farmworkers had cottages which they could live in for as long as they kept their job. Farmworkers without special skills were taken on for a day at a time.

Source A

You cannot go far along country roads just now without meeting wagons piled up with the goods and chattels [*belongings*] of farm hands changing quarters. They have been to some hiring fair and have got fresh places and here they are jogging about the country with their tables and chairs and beds and boxes and wives and children heaped up on the new master's wagon.

This was written in *Life in Our Villages* **by the Special Correspondent on the** *Daily News* **in 1891.**

Farmworkers often changed jobs. They went to hiring fairs in country towns. The tenant farmers inspected them. They hired the ones they wanted. Then the farmworkers and their families had to move to another cottage.

This photograph of a blacksmith was taken in about 1900. There were over 100,000 blacksmiths working in Britain. They were skilled workers. They usually had their own smithy where they worked. Sometimes they worked in the smithy on a large estate. Their main job was to put iron shoes on to the hooves of farm horses. Most blacksmiths also made the metal parts of farm tools. They made, for example, shepherds' crooks and ploughshares. Some blacksmiths made fancy wrought iron for gates and lanterns, and mended pots and pans.

Shepherds, too, were skilled workmen. They had to know everything about the sheep they kept. They had to know what to feed them with when the grass was not good enough; they had to know how to look after them during lambing; they had to **worm** them and cure them of foot rot; they had to look after them throughout the whole year.

In the same way, cowmen looked after their cows. They had to know what sorts of feed to give them. They had to fatten them up for beef, or make sure they made plenty of milk. They had to look after them when they were **pregnant** and when their calves were very young. Only a skilled man could do this.

6 Iron and cotton workers

Source A

Iron workers

Iron workers worked hard in dangerous conditions. Some of them had to be very skilful if the iron was to be made properly. First the iron ore was smelted: the men heated it in a furnace until the ore was so hot it turned liquid. Melted rocks and stones were left behind when they poured the liquid iron out into moulds. Sometimes, while the iron was setting, men hammered it hard to get all the impurities out. The iron made like this was called wrought iron. It was ready to be made into all kinds of things.

Products from iron

The Victorians made ships, bridges, guns, nails, steam engines and railway lines from iron. The iron industry helped make Britain a prosperous country.

This is a picture of an iron works at Poplar, London. It shows iron workers pouring hot, liquid iron into moulds. The picture was printed in *The Illustrated London News* in 1863.

Source B

The heat of the furnaces is terrible and the work is exhausting. The men have to wring out their clothes when they go home. The work is unhealthy and dangerous. Disease carries the men off at an early age. 'The work affects you all over,' said a worker to me, 'You get so cold that you shivers so that you can't hold your food. The furnaces burn your insides out of you.' The man had burns all over his body.

This was written by Robert Sherard, a journalist, after he had visited an iron works in 1897. He wrote it in his book, *The White Slaves of England*.

Cotton works

Men, women and children worked in cotton mills. Most cotton mills were in Lancashire. The adults worked the machinery. Some of them had to be skilled in working machinery and in making sure that the cotton thread did not break. The children crawled under the machinery taking out the fluff. Some of them, because they had small fingers, tied the cotton threads together when they broke. All this had to be done while the machinery was still moving.

Making cotton cloth

The cotton first had to be spun into thread. The spinning was usually done by a machine called a spinning mule. This made thread which was strong and of a good quality. The thread then had to be woven. This was done by power looms. After about 1840 the power to work the spinning mule and the looms came from steam engines.

Source C

The place was full of women, young, all of them, some large with child and obliged to stand twelve hours each day. Their hours are from five in the morning to seven in the evening, two hours of that being for rest. The heat was excessive, the stink pestiferous. The young women were all pale, thin, all with bare feet.

J. A. Roebuck visited a Glasgow cotton mill in 1897. He wrote about what he saw there. This is part of what he wrote.

This is a picture of cotton workers at a mill near Manchester.

Source D

7 Merchant sailors and fishermen

Working at sea

In 1841 there was a **census** in Britain. Everybody was counted. People had to give information about themselves to the census **enumerators** who visited every house. Because of the census we know that there were 7,002 **merchant sailors** living in London, and thousands more living in ports and harbours all round Britain. Some of these sailors were skilled men. Sailors like the ship's carpenter, the **bo'sun**, the **navigator** and the captain had special skills needed to sail the ship and keep it safe. The ordinary sailors who stacked **cargo** in the holds, turned the sails, scrubbed the decks, coiled ropes, pumped out the **bilges** and did routine jobs around a ship had no special skills. They were more like the labourers on land.

Fishermen

Fishermen, too, went to sea in ships. The difference between them and merchant sailors was that they did not carry cargo from port to port; they rarely travelled long distances, but kept to the fishing grounds around the coast of Britain. Some fishermen were skilled and some were not. All of them, however, had to be able to handle the heavy rope nets and the slippery fishy catch. There were hundreds of small fishing ports and villages around the coast of Britain. Whitby, in Yorkshire, was one of them. Whitby fishermen caught cod, haddock, plaice, halibut, hake, herring, mackerel and turbot. They caught crabs and lobsters, too.

Source A

Source B

The man at the mast-head sings out, 'There she blows – a whale in sight!' All the boats are lowered. In each boat are about three harpoons and two drags; the drag is to secure a whale until he can be got at – if the men are busy with another whale – and killed with the harpoon. The boat steerer, who rows first oar of the boat, drives his harpoon into a sperm whale. When struck, the whale will often seize a boat with his teeth, and turn it over with his tail. No boat is lowered after sundown, because it is unsafe. But the danger is great at all times.

This is part of what a ship's carpenter told Henry Mayhew about whale fishing in the South Seas. It was published in the *Morning Chronicle* in March 1850.

This photograph was taken by Frank Meadow Sutcliffe in the 1890s. It shows part of the Cornish fishing fleet moored at Whitby. Every year the Cornish fishermen caught mackerel and pilchards off the coast of Cornwall. The fleet then sailed north into the Irish Sea for herring. The ships then cut through the Caledonian Canal into the North Sea, and followed the herring south. The Cornish fishing fleet landed lots of herring at Whitby in September and October each year.

A dangerous life

All men who went to sea had to cope with sudden storms and hidden rocks that could wreck a ship. Perhaps the cargo of a merchant ship would shift and make the ship **list** dangerously. Perhaps the fish could not be found. Then the fishing boats would sail further and further away from their home port into unknown seas. Some ships were badly looked after by their owners. They leaked badly and had rotten sails. Going to sea was a dangerous business.

Lifeboats could only reach ships that were in trouble close to the shore. The rest had to manage as best they could. Hundreds of fishermen and merchant seamen drowned at sea. By 1852 Whitby was linked by the York and North Midland Railway to York and Leeds and, from Leeds, to the whole of the rail network. This meant that fish from Whitby could be sent by train to most of the big inland cities. Many people in cities like Derby, Leicester and Rugby ate fresh fish for the first time.

8 Servants

In 1851 there were over a million servants in Britain. 905,000 were women and girls and 134,000 were boys and men. Many worked in large houses owned by rich people. Some of them worked for people who did not earn a lot of money – just enough to employ one girl to do the hard work. Whoever they worked for, and whatever work they did, the job of servants was to make life easier for the people who employed them.

In large houses, the butler was in charge of the male servants and the housekeeper was in charge of the female servants. The servants had their own bedrooms at the top of the house, and a servants' hall where they ate their meals and relaxed when they had time to spare. Servants had to use special back stairs and corridors so they didn't often see the people they worked for.

Women servants

Cooks, kitchen maids and scullery maids worked in the kitchens, making meals and washing up. Housemaids looked after different rooms, cleaning, sweeping, dusting and clearing the grates. Laundry maids washed, scrubbed and ironed clothes. Nursery maids looked after the babies and young children.

Men servants

Men servants did different sorts of jobs. The valet looked after the clothes of the master of the house and saw that he was correctly dressed at all times. The butler looked after the wines and saw that meals were served properly. Footmen answered the door and carried messages. They went with the ladies of the house on walks, visits and carriage rides.

Source A

A valet	£60 a year
A house porter	£30 a year
A butler	£100 a year
Two footmen	£32 a year each
A steward's room boy	£18 a year
A housekeeper	£40 a year
A cook	£60 a year
A lady's maid	£22 a year
Two kitchen maids	£18 a year each
A scullery maid	£12 a year
A nurse	£36 a year
A nursemaid	£29 a year
Seven housemaids, paid £20, £18, £16, £14, three at £12	
Four laundry maids at £22, £16, two at £10	
Two stillroom maids paid at £16 and £12	

In 1871 these servants worked in the Earl of Leicester's country home of Holkham Hall. By looking at their wages we can work out which servants he thought were the most important.

I got a place where there were nine children. I was about fourteen then. I earned two shillings a week. I used to get up and light the fire, bath them and dress them and get their breakfast. I'd take them all out for a walk on the common. Then there was dinner to wash up and then by that time it would be tea time again. And then I had to put the children to bed and bath them and clean up the rooms and see to the fires. And then there would be the gentleman's supper to get. I wasn't in bed till twelve and I'd be up by six.

A woman remembers what her second job as a servant was like. This account was published in *The Cornhill Magazine* in May 1874.

This picture is called *The Morning After the Party*. **The rich people who had been at the party will probably still be in bed. The maid has to clear up the mess they made.**

9 Navvies

What did they do?

In 1845 there were about 200,000 navvies in Britain. After this, their numbers fell. This was because they had finished building many railway lines. It was the navvies who did most of the hard work involved in building the railways. Victorians called them the 'kings of the labourers'. This was because they were **specialists**. They **blasted** tunnels through solid rock. They built huge viaducts which carried rail tracks high above rivers. They lined dripping tunnels with clay bricks. They dug **cuttings** through different sorts of land so the rail track could run as flat and straight as possible.

Danger, death and injury

Navvies' work was dangerous. Some were killed and injured as they worked. One of the things they had to do was to clear away tonnes of earth and rocks. They usually did this by undermining. Gangs of navvies burrowed away, undermining great banks of soil and rock, until the overhanging mass of mud and rocks collapsed. If the navvies weren't quick enough getting away, they were buried alive. The Woodhead tunnel runs for nearly five kilometres through the Pennines between Sheffield and Manchester. It was dug between 1839 and 1845. Thirty-two navvies died building it. As well as the dead, there were 23 complicated broken arms and legs, 74 simple breaks, and another 140 serious cases,

including burns, cuts and **dislocations**. A navvy who was injured could not work and could not earn money. A navvy who was dead had probably had a wife and children depending on what he earned to keep them from starvation. Some navvies died because they took stupid risks. Three of them were killed playing a crazy game of follow-my-leader which ended up with them trying to jump across a huge shaft leading down to the Kilsby tunnel on the London to Birmingham line. The large numbers of deaths and accidents were so serious that in 1846 Parliament held an **enquiry**.

Pay in 1846

Navvies were not always paid money for their work. The **contractors**, who gave them jobs, often paid them with tickets. These tickets could be swapped at **tommy-shops** for ale, boots, bread, bacon, tobacco, shovels, jackets and many other goods. The problem was that the contractors owned the tommy-shops. They charged high prices in tickets, and so made a **profit** out of the navvies who worked for them.

Source
B

I went round by Eston. We call it the slaughterhouse, you know, because every day nearly there's an accident, and nigh every week, at the farthest, a death. Well, I stood and looked down, and there were a lot of chaps, ever so far below, and the cuttings so narrow. And a lot of stone fell, it was always falling, they were bound to be hurt. There was no room to get away nor mostly no warning. One chap I saw killed while I was there. So I said, 'Good money's all right, but I'd sooner keep my head on.' So I never asked for work, but came away again.

A navvy told Elizabeth Garnett why he refused work on a railway cutting. Elizabeth Garnett started the Christian Excavators' Union in 1875. Ten years later there were only 296 members out of around 70,000 navvies.

This is a painting of navvies digging a cutting for the London to Birmingham railway line. The line was finished in 1838. J. C. Bourne made a series of paintings while the line was being built. This one was painted in 1837. You can see that the navvies worked in separate gangs, yet all the gangs are together digging the cutting. The gang leader, called the ganger, said the gang would get the work done in a certain time. For this, each gang was paid an agreed amount. When the job was done, the navvies tramped to another one.

10 Farm labourers

In 1837, when Queen Victoria came to the throne, most men, women and children in Britain lived in the countryside. Over one million of these were farm labourers. They dug ditches and mended fences, ploughed fields and **mucked out** yards, sowed seeds and **reaped** hay, and did the hundred and one labouring jobs that had to be done. Nearly half a million people, usually women, worked indoors on farms. These women made cheeses and butter, milked cows and goats, smoked bacon and hams, baked bread, brewed ale and made cider. From 1861 fewer and fewer people worked on the land.

Working conditions

Farm labourers worked from six in the morning to six in the evening in summer. In winter they worked from dawn until dusk. The busiest time was harvest-time, whether it was corn or apples or hops that were being gathered in. There was plenty of money, plenty of ale and plenty of fun.

Gangs

Women and children sometimes worked in gangs under a **foreman.** Gang working was quite usual in eastern England, though it didn't often happen in other areas.

Source
A

The foreman agreed a price with a farmer for doing a job, and the gang would set to work. This job could be almost any sort of farm work: digging potatoes, clearing stones from a field or picking fruit, for example. Sometimes gangs were taken to their work in the farmer's wagon; usually they had to tramp along lanes and across fields to get there. Like all farmworkers, they worked in all weather – ice, snow and rain, and in the summer heat.

In 1867 a Gangs Act was passed by Parliament. It said that no child under eight could work in a gang. All gang foremen, too, had to get a special certificate saying they were of good character before they could work.

Source B

'Hand work is best work,' my master used to say. Corn was cut with a short **badging hook** and hay was cut with the **scythe**. A man could cut half an acre of corn a day and bind it into **sheaves**.

How country folk laughed when the first machines appeared. Some mowing machines had reaping gear fixed to them and were used as reapers, with a dozen men following behind binding the cut corn. There were a few threshing machines, but corn was mostly threshed by flail.

When I was seventeen I earned £16 a year and my keep. Bread was 3d a **quartern** loaf, milk 3d a quart, tobacco 3d an ounce, while beer was 2d a pint, the best was 3d.

Tom Mullins was a farmworker born in about 1863. When he was old he told J. H. Ingram what farm work had been like in the 1880s. J. H. Ingram wrote down what Tom Mullins told him. This is part of what he wrote.

Source C

Eight appears to be the ordinary age at which children join the gang, though seven is not unusual. One little girl, only four years old, was carried by her father to the fields and put to work. When the gangs are working a distance from home the children leave as early as five in the morning and do not return until eight at night. A little boy, only six years old, often walked more than six miles to work and often came home so tired that he could hardly stand. In winter the children often return from the fields crying from cold.

This account of children working in gangs was published in *The Quarterly Review* in 1867.

This picture, called *A Lincolnshire Gang*, was painted by Robert Walter Macbeth in 1876.

11 Coal miners

In Victorian times more and more coal was needed. It was needed to provide the steam power to drive more and more machinery. Coal mines were dug deeper and deeper, and life for the men, women and children working in them became more and more dangerous.

Down the mines

Men and boys usually worked as hewers. They worked in narrow tunnels. Some of the tunnels were only 45 cm high. Their job was to cut the coal from the coal face with picks.

As they worked they had to make sure that the roof of the coal seam didn't fall in on them. Sometimes they left columns of coal to support the roof; sometimes they used wooden pit props to hold it up. These did not always work and many miners were buried alive.

Women worked as drawers. It was their job to move the coal from the coal face to the bottom of the shaft. Miners put the coal in wooden trucks and the women dragged the trucks to the shafts. Carriers hauled the coal up to the surface in enormous buckets.

This picture of an explosion in a coal mine is called *Firedamp!* It shows what happens when dangerous gases ignite in a mine.

This photograph of colliery girls was taken at Wigan in Lancashire. An Act of Parliament in 1842 (the Mines Act) said that women and girls could not work underground. From that time they worked above ground, shovelling coal. Many people tried to stop them doing even this. They said that the work was too hard and was not suitable for women. Most colliery girls enjoyed their work and wanted to carry on doing it. In 1887 the government said it would not stop the women being colliery girls, if that was what they wanted.

I have a belt round my waist, and a chain passing between my legs, and I go on my hands and feet. The tunnel is very steep and we have to hold by a rope. I have drawn [pulled trucks] till I have the skin off me; the belt and chain are worse when we are in the family way [pregnant].

In 1840 the government set up a Royal Commission to find out about the work people did in coal mines. This is what Betty Harris, who was 37 years old, told them. She worked as a drawer in a pit in Little Bolton.

12 Casual workers

In Victorian times there were thousands and thousands of workers who did not have regular jobs. They worked when they could and where they could. These were labourers like the dock-workers, porters, street-cleaners and house-painters. They were workers like the knife-grinders, window-menders, **pedlars** and pie-makers. Women worked as cleaners and did other people's washing. They could never be sure from day to day whether they would earn any money. A chair-mender, for example, might not find anybody who had chairs they wanted mended. In good times there would be work for most of the year. In bad times, like the 1830s and 1840s, most **casual workers** nearly starved.

This is a photograph of workmen shovelling Thames mud out of a dredger. At this time the East and West India docks at Blackwall and the Isle of Dogs had to be dredged. Mud had to be taken away so that ships could get in to the docks. The mud was dumped on marshes lower down the River Thames at Crossness. Most of the mud was taken out of the dredgers by buckets. The mud left at the very bottom of the dredgers had to be shovelled out by workmen. Thousands of Londoners used the river Thames as a **sewer**. Workmen shovelling this kind of mud and muck not only worked in smelly, filthy conditions. They also ran the risk of catching all sorts of diseases.

This picture is called *The Old Chair-mender*. It is a wood **engraving** and was made by the Dalziel brothers in 1863. The woman in the cottage has given the chair-mender a broken chair. He is weaving a new seat for it using the **rushes** on the ground in front of him.

Source
C

It was distress (poverty) that first drove me to it. I had learnt to make willow bonnets, but that branch of trade went entirely out. So, having a wife and children, I wrote a paper. I got it printed and took it out into the streets and sold it. I did very well with it and made 5s a day while it lasted. I was never brought up to any mechanical trade. My father was a clergyman. It breaks my heart when I think of it. I would give the world to get out of my present life. It would be heaven to get away from the place where I am.

In Victorian times almost anything could be bought on the streets. Here a street-seller explains to Henry Mayhew how he came to be doing his job. The paper he wrote is called a 'broadside'. Street-sellers sold thousands of different broadsides. The broadsides gave people news and information, stories and songs. They sold for around a halfpenny each.

13 Children at work

Children of poor parents began working for money when they were very young. Every penny counted, and so it was important that children began working as soon as they could earn something, no matter how little. As soon as a child could do things like stitch neatly, weed a row of vegetables, collect fluff from underneath moving machines or throw stones at crows that were eating corn seeds, their parents set them to do it every day. This meant that some children began working when they were as young as three or four years old. Many employers were very strict. They made the children work long hours. They did not allow them to talk or have breaks for play. Many employers whipped children if they worked too slowly or broke any rules.

Source B

I go about the streets with watercresses crying, 'Four bunches a penny! Watercresses!' I am eight years old. On and off I've been near a twelve month on the streets. Sometimes I make a great deal of money. One day I took one shilling and sixpence and the cresses cost sixpence. But it isn't often I get such luck as that. I oftener makes threepence or fourpence. I don't have no dinner. Mother gives me two slices of bread and butter and a cup of tea for breakfast and then I go till tea and has the same.

This is what a girl watercress seller told Henry Mayhew about her work. He wrote it down and published it in 1851 in his book, *London Labour and the London Poor*.

Source A

This is a picture of Lord Shaftesbury visiting the coal mines in the Black Country, 1840–2. Lord Shaftesbury worked hard to persuade Parliament that children's working conditions had to be made better.

Source C

This picture shows children working in a brickworks. They had to carry huge lumps of clay on their heads. They took the clay to the sheds where men began working it to start the brick-making process. The children had to carry the finished bricks to where they were stacked ready for builders to collect them. The work was hard. Children in brickworks walked up to sixteen kilometres a day carrying heavy loads. They did this in the hot summer sun and in the freezing cold of winter.

Members of Parliament were worried about the long hours worked by children. In the 1830s and 1840s they set up several Commissions into the sorts of work done by children. They passed Acts of Parliament which they hoped would improve things. For example, in 1842 the Mines Act said that no girls were allowed to work down mines, and that boys had to be ten years old before they could work underground. In 1847 Parliament passed an Act which said that children were not allowed to work for more than ten hours a day in **textile** mills. In 1875 **sweeps** were forbidden to use climbing boys. Some people thought that the government should not tell employers what they could and could not do with their workers. Others said that the government should protect people like children who did not have the power to look after themselves at work.

Source D

The flesh must be hardened. This is done by rubbing it, chiefly on the elbows and knees, with the strongest brine. You must stand over them with a cane or coax them by a promise or a halfpenny if they will stand a few more rubs. At first they will come back from their work with their arms and knees streaming with blood and the knees looking as if the caps had been pullèd off. Then they must be rubbed with brine again and perhaps go off at once to another chimney.

George Ruff, a sweep from Nottingham, explained how he toughened up the knees and elbows of climbing boys by rubbing them with salt water. He told this to a Parliamentary Commission in 1863. Sweeps sent small boys up tall, twisting chimneys, where brushes could not go, to sweep the soot down.

GLOSSARY

aristocracy people from noble families where the men sat in the House of Lords and who were earls, dukes and barons

badging hook a sharp hook, about 0.5 metre in diameter, with a wooden handle, used for cutting corn by hand

bankers owners or managers of banks

bilges the nearly flat part of a ship's bottom which often fills with water

blast blow up with explosives

bo'sun a ship's officer in charge of the crew

cargo goods carried in a ship's hold

casual worker someone who works irregularly, taking what jobs they can get

census An official count of number of people in a country. In Britain in the 19th century there was a census every ten years.

climate the weather

commercial travellers people who travel the country for a manufacturer, selling the manufacturer's goods to shops so that they can sell them to their customers

contractor a person who agrees to build a railway line

cutting part of the land around a railway line which has been cut away so that the railway line runs flat

dislocation when a joint, like a shoulder, hip or knee, is pulled or pushed out of place

engraving a design or picture cut out of wood or metal

enquiry an investigation where people try to find out the facts about something

enumerator a person who collects information for a census

foreman a workman in charge of other workmen

hedging and ditching farm work involving cutting hedges back into shape and clearing ditches

House of Lords part of parliament which is made up of all the dukes, earls, bishops and barons and which has to agree to Bills sent to them by the House of Commons before they can become law

infections diseases and illnesses

invest put money into a business, mill or factory

ironmasters men who own iron foundries

lavished give or spend a great deal

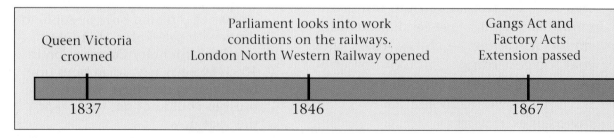

Queen Victoria crowned — 1837

Parliament looks into work conditions on the railways. London North Western Railway opened — 1846

Gangs Act and Factory Acts Extension passed — 1867

lawyers barristers and solicitors: people trained to know about the law

list tip over to one side

merchant a person who trades, usually with foreign countries

merchant sailors sailors who work on ships that carry cargoes

muck out shovel all the muck out of a farmyard, stable or cowshed

navigator a sailor who is skilled in using instruments to work out the direction in which the ship should be sailing

pedlars people who walk around streets and villages selling goods they carry with them

peer a man who is a member of the House of Lords

pregnant expecting a baby

profit money made from buying and selling

quartern a special sized loaf of bread

reap to cut for harvest

rent money paid to a landlord for land or a house or cottage

respectable honest and decent

rushes tough grasses that grow near water

scythe a long thin curved blade at the end of a long handle used for cutting corn

sewer a pipe taking waste away from a lavatory or sink

sheaf (pl sheaves) a bundle of corn stalks tied together after reaping

specialists people who have a lot of detailed knowledge about the job they are doing

status rank or social position of a person

sweep a person who sweeps soot from chimneys

tenant farmers farmers who rent their farms from landlords

textile fabric

tommy-shops shops where workers can swap tokens for goods

working conditions what it's like at work: the hours, building, noise, danger

worm giving animals like sheep a medicine to kill the worms in their gut

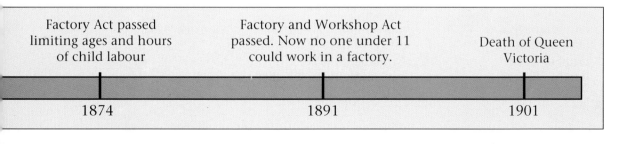

Factory Act passed limiting ages and hours of child labour	Factory and Workshop Act passed. Now no one under 11 could work in a factory.	Death of Queen Victoria
1874	1891	1901

INDEX

Plain numbers (3) refer to the text and written sources. Italic numbers (3) refer to a picture.